REV. DR. MEL WHITE'S

WHAT THE BIBLE SAYS—AND DOESN'T SAY—ABOUT HOMOSEXUALITY

A REPLY, REFUTATION AND REBUTTAL

BY

JOHN TELLER

TIME BOOKS

What the Bible Says—and Doesn't Say—About Homosexuality:
A Reply, Refutation and Rebuttal

ISBN (13) (Paperback): 978-1-68109-012-2
ISBN (10) (Paperback): 1-68109-012-0
ISBN (13) (Kindle): 978-1-68109-013-9
ISBN (10) (Kindle): 1-68109-013-9
ISBN (13) (ePub): 978-1-68109-014-6
ISBN (10) (ePub): 1-68109-014-7

Time Books™
an imprint of TellerBooks™
TellerBooks.com/Time_Books

www.TellerBooks.com

Manufactured in the U.S.A.

NOTE: Unless otherwise stated herein, all biblical Scriptures quoted herein are taken from the New King James Version or American Standard Version translations, unless the verses are quoted directly from the Rev. Dr. White's book, in which case other translations may be used.

DISCLAIMER: The opinions, views, positions and conclusions expressed in this volume reflect those of the individual author and not necessarily those of the publisher or any of its imprints, editors or employees.

CONTENTS

ABBREVIATIONS

English Translations of the Bible:

ASV...............American Standard Version
BBE...............Bible in Basic English
Darby.............Darby Bible
ESV ....English Standard Version
ISV ....International Standard Version
KJV ....King James Version
MKJV............Modern King James Version
NIV ....New International Version
NKJV ....New King James Version
RSV...............Revised Standard Version

Books of the Bible:

1Ch.................1 Chronicles
1Co.................1 Corinthians
1Jn..................1 John
1Ki.................1 Kings
1Pe.................1 Peter
1Sa.................1 Samuel
1Th ....1 Thessalonians
1Ti.................1 Timothy
2Ch.................2 Chronicles
2Co ....2 Corinthians
2Jn.................2 John
2Ki.................2 Kings
2Pe.................2 Peter
2Sa.................2 Samuel
2Th ....2 Thessalonians
2Ti ....2 Timothy
3Jo ....3 John
Acts ....Book of Acts
Amos ....Book of Amos
Col.................Colossians
Dan.................Daniel
Deu.................Deuteronomy

Ecc.................Ecclesiastes
Eph ....Ephesians
Est ....Esther
Exo ....Exodus
Eze.................Ezekiel
Ezr ....Book of Ezra
Gal.................Galatians
Gen.................Genesis
Hab.................Habakkuk
Hag.................Haggai
Heb.................Hebrews
Hos ....Hosea
Isa.................Isaiah
Jas.................James
Jer.................Jeremiah
Job ....Book of Job
Joel ....Book of Joel
John.................Gospel of John
Jon ....Jonah
Jos ....Joshua
Jude ....Book of Jude
Jdg ....Judges
Lam ....Lamentations
Lev ....Leviticus
Luke ....Gospel of Luke
Mal ....Malachi
Mark.................Gospel of Mark
Mat ....Gospel of Matthew
Mic ....Micah
Nah.................Nahum
Neh.................Nehemiah
Num.................Numbers
Oba.................Obadiah
Phm ....Philemon
Php ....Philippians
Pro ....Proverbs
Psa ....Psalms
Rev ....Revelation
Rom.................Romans
Ruth.................Book of Ruth

Son ....Song of Solomon
Tit....................Titus
Zec..................Zechariah
Zep ....Zephaniah

CHAPTER 1. INTRODUCTION

In "What the Bible Says - And Doesn't Say - About Homosexuality," Dr. Mel White argues that the Hebrew and Christian Scriptures, when correctly understood, neither condemn nor prohibit homosexual relationships between two loving, committed partners. The apparent prohibitions of sodomy and other homosexual acts in the Old Testament are intended not as injunctions from God, but rather, as reflections of societal tastes and preferences. In any event, the prohibitions and societal preferences of the Old Testament have no place in the new covenant of grace, and therefore should have little bearing on the conduct of contemporary Christians. As for the apparent prohibitions of homosexual conduct in the New Testament, these are mostly based on mistranslations that misunderstand the original text. The term "homosexual" used in Paul's Epistles has no modern English equivalent, and is best rendered as the sexual exploitation of "effeminate call boys" by old men, not homosexuality between two men or two women in committed, loving relationships. Only in translations rendered after the mid-twentieth century did the term "homosexuality" begin to erroneously appear as a reflection of societal prejudices against homosexuals.

First, it must be conceded that Dr. White does make some strong points, such as his argument that the word "homosexual" in 1Corinthians 6:9 and 1 Timothy 1:10 first only appeared in English translations as "homosexual" in 1958. In other areas, however, Dr. White's pamphlet is based on broad assumptions and a rejection of the divine inspiration of the Scriptures.

CHAPTER 2. MISUNDERSTANDING THE DIVINE INSPIRATION OF THE SCRIPTURES

Looking at the Old Testament's apparent injunctions against homosexual relations, Dr. White holds that we "miss what these passages say about God when we spend so much time debating what they say about sex." He goes on to examine the condemnations of same-sex relations in the Old Testament, such as Leviticus 18:22[1,2] and Leviticus 20:13.[3] Dr. White argues that to read these as condemnations or prohibitions of homosexual relations is a misinterpretation, for these passages are not intended as absolute statutes written by God on how men and women should treat and relate to one another; rather, they represent a "holiness code," or "list of behaviors that people of faith find offensive in a certain place and time." These statutes reflect a Jewish culture that found same-sex unions to be offensive.

Dr. White here commits several errors. First, he repeats constantly that these injunctions against homosexual relations

---

[1] All Scriptures are taken from the New International Version® (NIV) (copyright © 1973, 1978, 1984 Biblica. All rights reserved. The "NIV" and "New International Version" trademarks are registered in the United States Patent and Trademark Office by Biblica), unless otherwise indicated.

[2] "You shall not lie with a male as one lies with a female. It is an abomination."

[3] "A man who sleeps with another man is an abomination and should be executed."

represent a code that the Jews found offensive, as though this code is nothing more than a list of preferences of the Jewish people. He characterizes this code to a pact to which he bound himself as a high school student: "I don't drink, smoke, or chew, or go with girls who do." Dr. White misses, however, the first premise of orthodox Christianity: the Hebrew Scriptures were written by God through inspired prophets, not by individuals seeking to record cultural preferences. The Scriptures that Dr. White quotes were given to Moses by God: "Then the LORD spoke to Moses, saying [Lev 18:1] … You shall not lie with a male as with a woman [Lev 18:22]" and again in Leviticus 20: "Then the LORD spoke to Moses, saying [Lev 20:1] … If a man lies with a male as he lies with a woman, both of them have committed an abomination [Lev 20:13]." Thus, when homosexuality is prohibited in the Jewish law, we must read this as God's injunction, not as man's injunction.

Yet Dr. White claims just a few paragraphs later that an abomination in the Hebrew Scriptures is a behavior that "people in a certain time and place consider tasteless or offensive." Here, Dr. White essentially ignores the preface "Then the LORD spoke to Moses …," and can only do so if he denies that the Scriptures are divinely inspired, perfect and complete. This denial of the divine inspiration of Scripture can only be true if Leviticus 18:22 ("You shall not lie with a male as one lies with a female") were written by Jews of the time reflecting their cultural preferences. Yet if this were the case, then Leviticus 18:1 ("the LORD spoke to Moses, saying …") cannot be true. It must be fabricated if God is not the author. And if Dr. White believes the verse to be fabricated, then in what way does he "take the Bible seriously"? Certainly not as an orthodox Christian who believes the Bible to be the perfect, unaltered and true Word of the living God.

Dr. White's discussion of Genesis 38:9-10 similarly reveals this problem. The verses state that Onan "spilled his seed on the ground," and that "the thing which Onan did displeased *the Lord*" (emphasis added). It does not state that the thing displeased the Jewish writers of the text; it states clearly that it displeased the Lord. Yet this is not the point that Dr. White takes from the text. Rather, he interprets the text to mean that for "Jewish writers of Scripture," masturbation or the interruption of coitus was "an abomination (and one worthy of death)." He clearly misses that if the Bible is the true and unaltered Word of God, it was God who was offended by Onan's act.

If Dr. White took the Scripture seriously (in the sense of believing it to be true), then there would be no question as to what the Jewish writers of Scripture found to be displeasing or offensive. When the Scripture says that "the thing which Onan did displeased the Lord," the discussion would end there, with no discussion of whether the spilling of semen was displeasing to the Jewish author, since the text does not state "the thing which Onan did displeased this author." He would accept with faith that the Scripture, divinely inspired by God and wholly true, displeased God; otherwise, he would have to believe that the Bible is at best partially accurate and partially corrupted by human experience, culture, the preferences of the writers, etc.

Of course, there are verses in the Scripture that support the notion that homosexuality was judged by the Jews as sinful. For example, in the book of Judges, when the men of the city came to the master of the house demanding that he bring out his guest that they may "know him carnally" (Jdg 19:22), the master implored them not to "act so wickedly" (Jdg 19:23). If all of the Scripture's references to homosexuality were expressed in this way as the private judgment of individual actors, then there would be no reason to object to Dr. White's arguments. Yet the Bible states clearly that homosexuality gravely displeased God in addition to these individual actors.

CHAPTER 3. THE OLD TESTAMENT LAW AS INAPPLICABLE TO MODERN SOCIETY

A. OVERVIEW

Dr. White's next argument is that the Old Testament Law was abrogated by Jesus and Paul and is no longer applicable to Gentile Christians. Dr. White writes, "Jesus and Paul both said the holiness code in Leviticus [which appears to condemn homosexuality] does not pertain to Christian believers." The "holiness code" is, according to Dr. White, largely irrelevant and outdated, and includes prohibitions on, among other things, "round haircuts [Lev 19:27], tattoos [Lev 19:28], working on the Sabbath [Exo 23:12], wearing garments of mixed fabrics [Lev 19:19], eating pork or shellfish [Lev 11:7-12]," or playing with pigskins, as in football (Lev 11:8 prohibits eating the flesh of swine or touching their carcasses). Dr. White is correct here in some respects but his statements are overbroad and thus inaccurate.

B. THE OLD TESTAMENT LAW WITH ISRAEL

It is first important to understand the nature of the Old Testament Law. It was given to Moses by God as part of a Covenant between God and the nation of Israel. It was never intended as binding on all peoples. When God became man through Christ, a New Covenant was established through which all who profess Christ as Savior would be saved. The Covenant was not restricted to any one people or ethnicity. Nor was it based on obedience to the Old Testament Law. Just as the Old Testament established a Covenant by Law, the New Testament formed a Covenant through Grace.

C. WAS THE OLD TESTAMENT LAW ABROGATED?

This should not, however, be taken to mean that the Old Testament Law was abrogated. Christ states that "until heaven and earth disappear, not the smallest letter, not the least stroke of a pen, will by any means disappear from the Law until everything is accomplished" (Mat 5:18). The Law continues to stand as the means to Salvation, yet because all have fallen short of the Law and have sinned (Isa 53:6; Rom 3:10), God has provided a gate to Salvation through Christ's fulfillment of the Law in his perfect, sinless life and Atonement. Christ thus proclaims: "Do not think that I have come to abolish the Law or the Prophets; I have not come to abolish them but to fulfill them" (Mat 5:17).

It is important to discern the difference between the letter of the Law and the spirit of the Law. God is concerned with the spirit of the law. Christ was displeased when the Pharisees and scribes placed all of their attention on the letter of the law while ignoring the spirit of the law. For example, he accused the scribes and Pharisees of paying "tithe of mint and anise and cummin, and [yet neglecting] the weightier matters of the law: justice and mercy and faith (Mat 23:23), and then says, "These you ought to have done, without leaving the others undone" (Mat 23:23). It thus does not suffice that one obey the outward dimensions of the Law; it is more important that he fulfill the spirit of the Law.

D. THE SPIRIT OF THE LAW

It therefore cannot be said, as Dr. White writes, that "Jesus and Paul both said the holiness code in Leviticus does not pertain to Christian believers." What can, however, be said is that the Old Testament Law applies to Christians in a different way. Christians are lifted to a higher standard. They are expected to obey the Law while not ignoring the weightier matters of the Law: justice and mercy and faith. The spirit of the Law becomes paramount over the letter of the Law. Thus, Christians are prohibited not only from the sin of murder, but also from being angry at one's brother (Mat 5:22). Similarly, it is not enough that Christians refrain from adultery; they must also refrain from even looking at a woman lustfully, for such is the equivalent of "adultery of the heart" (Mat 5:28).

E. HOW THEN CAN WE BE SAVED? THE COUNCIL OF JERUSALEM

Of course, no one but Christ can proclaim a sin-free life that has fulfilled both the letter and the spirit of the Law. This is why God has given the gift of grace. The Council of Jerusalem recognized and affirmed this. When some were teaching that the Gentile converts to Christianity were required to undergo circumcision and to follow other precepts of the Old Testament Law, the Council concluded that the Gentile converts were required only to "abstain from food sacrificed to idols, from blood, from the meat of strangled animals and from sexual immorality" (Act 15:29).

It would be easy to read this Council as having abrogated all of the Old Testament Law, with the exception of the four cited prohibitions. Yet such a rash reading would overlook the message of the Gospel. Taken with Christ's earlier-cited teachings, the Council did not intend to abrogate the Old Testament Law, but rather, to acknowledge that it was through God's Grace, not through the Law, that one could be saved. Rather than burden the Gentile converts with laws by which even the Jews could not abide, the Council decided to make only a small fraction of the law binding and to allow the lives of the converts to be guided to good fruit through the Holy Spirit.

The Council thus held that the Gentile converts would not be under the Old Testament's circumcision requirement. This is not because the Old Testament Law was abrogated. Rather, the disciples recognized Christ's teaching that what is paramount is the spirit of the Law. Christ seeks not outward, physical circumcision, but circumcision of the heart. With a heart turned towards God, the Old Testament circumcision requirement is fulfilled.

This is the approach that believers must take towards the Old Testament Law. The Church understood that the Laws still applied, but in a different way. Whereas in the Old Covenant, circumcision was an outward physical sign, in the New Covenant, it is of the heart. Just as the Old Testament Law is a forerunner of New Testament Grace, so too is outward, physical circumcision a forerunner to inward, spiritual circumcision.

Thus, one cannot write off so quickly the Old Testament Laws against homosexuality, just as one cannot write off those against round haircuts and the like. Each of these laws speaks to man's good, to his relationship with God and to his relationships with other people. Though the content of many of these laws may appear to be outdated and inapplicable to modern day society, the spirit behind them continues to work towards man's good.

For example, Leviticus 27-28 states: "Do not cut the hair at the sides of your head or clip off the edges of your beard. Do not cut your bodies for the dead or put tattoo marks on yourselves." These four prohibitions most likely deal with mourning rites: "The hair-cutting of verse 27 is probably associated with the skin-cutting in verse 28, and both were related to specific pagan rituals having to do with the dead. The description of the cuts made on the body 'for the dead' in verse 28 offers explicit support for this interpretation."[4] The ban on these rites cannot be understood without acknowledging the Jews' flirtation with idolatry: Leviticus 27-28 intends to ban idolatrous rites. The spirit of these laws is fulfilled when the believer worships the one true God and flees idolatry. Though the letter of the Law was given to Israel within a specific content, the spirit of the law continues to apply today. The same can be said of the entire code of the Old Testament; as Christ said with His own words, he came not to "abolish the Law or the Prophets ... but to fulfill them" (Mat 5:17).

F. DISTINGUISHING THE DIFFERENT FORMS OF LAW

Christians must thus discern the spirit of the Laws of the Old Testament in order to understand how they continue to apply in their lives. The Old Testament's sacrificial offering of animals had

---

[4] Rob Bowman, "Gay Marriage and the Haircut Argument," *in The Religious Researcher*, 11 Dec. 2009, available at http://www.religiousresearcher.org/2008/12/11/gay-marriage-and-the-haircut-argument/.

been fulfilled by the cross, because Christ's body was the final and ultimate sacrifice. The sacrifice of animals is thus no longer required of Christians, because the final sacrifice was made. Many of the hygienic laws of the Old Testament applied to Jews at a time when modern technologies did not exist. Although some of the dietary laws and prohibitions against mixed fabrics may appear outdated to modern ears, the spirit behind these Laws, which focus on being a good steward of one's body, continues to apply.

G. "SEXUAL IMMORALITY" AS HOMOSEXUAL RELATIONS

Yet even if Dr. White were correct and all of the laws outlined in the Old Testament were abrogated, homosexuality would still be prohibited on the basis of Acts 15:29, which requires believers to "abstain from … sexual immorality" (Act 15:29). As we will see below, sexual immorality to the writers of the New Testament included homosexual relations, because the writers of the New Testament repeatedly condemned homosexuality. The Council, in placing a continued banned on sexual immorality, reaffirmed and preserved the Old Testament's prohibition on homosexual relations.

CHAPTER 4. THE BIBLE: A BOOK ABOUT GOD OR "HUMAN SEXUALITY"?

Dr. White's next argument states that the biblical verses dealing with human sexuality speak *not* to the sexual relations between men and women, but rather, to God's holiness, since "the Bible is a book about God, not about human sexuality." These passages should therefore not be read as prohibitions on human sexual behavior.

A. THE COPERNICUS ARGUMENT

Dr. White first points to the heliocentric cosmology that some passages of the Bible appear to point towards (e.g., Joshua 10:13). He states that theologians of Copernicus's day, including Martin Luther, condemned Copernicus's heliocentric cosmology because they failed to understand that Joshua 10:13, like the rest of the Bible, is about *God, not* about astronomy. Because the Bible is not meant to deal with questions as to whether the earth revolves around the sun or vice versa, we should not condemn the theories of astrologists such as Copernicus that appear to contradict verses such as Joshua 10:13, because these verses in reality do not deal with astrology; they deal with God. Dr. White then draws a parallel to those verses that appear to condemn homosexuality: these passages are about God, not about human sexuality, and we should not take from these verses a blanket ban on homosexual relations.

Dr. White's analysis is flawed in two respects. The first is in its interpretation of Joshua 10:13. Although Dr. White is correct in pointing out that those who read Joshua 10:13 and related passages as evidence against Copernicus's heliocentric cosmology were mistaken in their reading, Dr. White's reading that the passage has *nothing* to do with astrology is similarly flawed. The passage correctly states that the sun stood still for a full day. It is important however to note that this passage describes what was perceived *from the perspective of the people perceiving the event*. To these people, the sun appeared not to move through the sky. This does not mean that the sun normally revolves around the earth, just as the expressions "the sun rose" and "the sun set" do not necessarily mean that the sun actually moves around the earth. Just as the concepts of sunset and sunrise could indicate that the sun stands still and the earth makes a full rotation each day, so too could the idea of the sun moving through the sky indicate the same thing. The fact that certain church authorities at the time of Copernicus interpreted the verse as counter to a heliocentric cosmology does not in itself mean that the verse has nothing to do with astrology or that the sun did not stand still from the human perspective.

B. THE BIBLE IS ABOUT GOD'S HOLINESS, WHICH HAS IMPLICATIONS OVER THE CONDUCT OF MANKIND

The second way in which Dr. White's analysis is flawed is that if followed to its natural conclusion, the Christian would deem all of the commandments that govern human relations to be irrelevant. If we conclude like Dr. White that the Bible is a "book about God, not about human sexuality," then we could also state that it is also not about human anger, or human jealousy, or human dishonesty. If one would were to conclude that 1 Corinthians 6:9 dealt only with God, and not human sexuality, why would he not also conclude that Exodus 20:14, which prohibits adultery, was a commandment dealing only with God, and not human sexuality? If all of these commandments, from those given on Mount Sinai to those given in the Sermon on the Mount, do not concern the affairs of men, then they could all be equally ignored.

In reality, the Bible is about God's holiness, and God's holiness has implications over the conduct of mankind because we are created in God's image and are thus commanded to reflect His nature in holy, righteous, pure living. Part of living purely means fleeing sexual immorality. It is no wonder that in the Epistles alone, fornication and other forms of sexual immorality are condemned half a dozen times (1Co 6:9-10; 1Co 6:13b, 18; 1Co 10:6-8; Gal 5:19-21; 1Th 4:3-5; Eph 5:1-3).[5]

---

[5] The term "fornication" is used in these verses in the King James Version. The term used varies in other translations.

CHAPTER 5. HOMOSEXUALITY IS ALSO BANNED IN THE NEW TESTAMENT

Dr. White's next focus is on the New Testament. Having argued that the Old Testament's bans on homosexuality were only cultural reflections and that the Old Testament Law was in any case abrogated, Dr. White is faced with the New Testament's bans against homosexual conduct. Here, his principal argument is that homosexuality was never banned in the New Testament; rather, sexually abusive relationships, of which "homosexuality" is a mistranslation, were condemned and prohibited. To evaluate whether Dr. White's arguments are persuasive, we will examine the three New Testament verses that he treats: Romans 1:26-27, 1 Corinthians 6:9, and 1 Timothy 1:10.

A. ROMANS 1:26-27

Romans 1:26-7 states: "For this reason God gave them up to vile passions. For even their women exchanged the natural use for what is against nature. Likewise also the men, leaving the natural use of the woman, burned in their lust for one another, men with men committing what is shameful."

Dr. Mel White, citing arguments made by Dr. Louis B. Smedes, argues that because the homosexuals refused to worship

God, God abandoned and gave them up to sexual immorality. Yet he has it backwards; it is not that these men and women succumbed to sexual immorality because they refused to worship God; rather, it is because they engaged in homosexual activities that God abandoned them. It is not that they sank into sexual depravity because they rejected God, but rather, God abandoned them because they engaged in homosexual activity. The text states, "For this reason God gave them up to vile passions. For even their women exchanged the natural use for what is against nature. Likewise also the men, leaving the natural use of the woman, burned in their lust for one another, men with men committing what is shameful" (Rom 1:26-7). "For this reason" refers to the actions of the following sentences: "For even their women exchanged the natural use for what is against nature ..." The text could just as easily read: "Because their women exchanged the natural use for what is against nature ..., God gave them up to vile passions."

Dr. White's interpretation is credible in some respects. Romans 1:23 describes the sins of idolatry of the godless, and is directly followed by, "Therefore God gave them over in the sinful desires of their hearts to sexual impurity for the degrading of their bodies with one another" (Romans 1:24). This makes it appear as though the homosexuality of the godless came about as a result of their own sins. Yet even this interpretation is not favorable to homosexuality: if homosexuality is a state that God delivers the depraved into as a result of their rejection of God, then is homosexuality a state to be desired? Whether it is a sin that causes God's abandonment of the sinner or a state brought about as a result of sin, homosexuality is a state to be avoided. Even if Dr. Smedes is granted his argument, and we conclude that "The people

Paul had in mind refused to acknowledge and worship God, and for this reason were abandoned by God. And being abandoned by God, they sank into sexual depravity," then the biblical text is equating sexual depravity with the homosexual exchange of "the natural use for what is against nature," thus equating homosexuality with sexual depravity.

B. FIRST CORINTHIANS 6:9 AND FIRST TIMOTHY 1:9-10

1. Introduction and Overview

First Corinthians 6:9 states: "Do you not know that the wicked will not inherit the kingdom of God? Do not be deceived: Neither the sexually immoral nor idolaters nor adulterers nor male prostitutes nor homosexual offenders." 1 Timothy 1:9-10 states: "We also know that the law is made not for the righteous but for lawbreakers and rebels, the ungodly and sinful, the unholy and irreligious, for those who kill their fathers or mothers, for murderers, 10 for the sexually immoral, for those practicing homosexuality, for slave traders and liars and perjurers. And it is for whatever else is contrary to the sound doctrine."[6]

Dr. White argues that these texts, which are often used as evidence of the Bible's condemnation of homosexuality, do not actually refer to homosexuality as we understand it. Rather, they refer to sexually abusive or perverted behavior. Only recently did

---

[6] This translation is taken from Today's New International Version. The NIV uses the term "perverts" in place of "homosexuals." Other translations that use "homosexuals" include the New American Standard Bible, the Contemporary English Version, the International Standard Version, God's Word Translation, the Holman Christian Standard Bible, Today's New International Version, and the Modern King James Version. The New Living Translation and the English Standard Version translate the term as men "who practice homosexuality."

translations of these texts begin to render the term as "homosexuality."

2. The Idea of Homosexuality is in the Scriptures, even if the Word "Homosexual" is not

a. Overview

Dr. White is correct in pointing out that starting only in 1958 did English-language translations of the Bible begin to use the word "homosexuality" in translations of 1 Corinthians 6:9 and 1 Timothy 1:9-10. However, it is important to note that it was only in 1864 that homosexuals were declared as a distinct class of individuals. Before this declaration by the German social scientist Karl Heinrich Ulrichs, homosexual acts were simply considered to be unnatural behaviors. After the declaration, the concept of homosexuality was introduced into social science. It took time—decades—for the idea to catch on and for the English language to adopt a term to describe the group. Prior to the twentieth century, "homosexual" was not a term used in English parlance. As the word "homosexual" became more common in English parlance, it was ultimately introduced into literature, writing, and ultimately, into translations of the Bible. The late use of the word "homosexuality" should thus not be used as evidence that earlier translations of the Scriptures did not condemn homosexual acts; rather, it serves only as evidence it took time for the modern term for the behavior was used and ultimately incorporated in modern translations.

Because heterosexuals were not known as a distinct group during the time of Paul and Moses, there was no word in Hebrew or Greek that referred to homosexuals. According to the Oxford English Dictionary, the first reference of the term "homosexual" in the English language appeared in C. G. Chaddock's 1892 translation of Krafft-Ebing's *Psychopathia Sexualis* III 255. The word simply was not used prior to that time. Thus, it is natural and expected that the term "homosexual" would not appear until English language translations of the mid-1900s. Yet although the term "homosexual" does not appear in earlier editions, the idea of "lying with a man as a man lies with a female" (Lev 18:22) is clearly banned in even the older English translations of the Scriptures.

Because the idea of homosexuality as an identity group only developed at the end of the Nineteenth Century, the word "homosexual" did not appear until the Nineteenth Century and was not popularized in the English language until the Twentieth Century. Given this history, it is no surprise that the term "homosexual" did not appear in English translations of the New Testament until the middle of the Twentieth Century. Language is dynamic, and as words come into existence, written texts will come to incorporate them.

Although the idea of a "homosexual" as an identity class or distinct group inclined towards sexual relations with the same gender did not exist in the days of Paul and Moses, the sexual behaviors in which homosexuals engage did exist and were clearly prohibited in the Scriptures.

b. History of the Term "Homosexuality"

Dr. White asserts that the use of the word "homosexual" only first appeared in the translations of the Scriptures in 1958, and "that translator made the decision for all of us that placed the word homosexual in the English-language Bible for the very first time." Dr. White then suggests that "the decision ... that placed the word homosexual in the English-language Bible for the very first time" reflects "society's prejudice and [desire to] condemn God's gay children."

I must respectfully disagree. Although the Scriptural translations prior to 1958 did not in fact use the word "homosexual," the idea of sexual relations with members of the same sex does appear in the pre-1958 scriptural translations. The use of the term "homosexual" does not reflect a sudden shift in society's prejudice against homosexuals; it is simply the same idea expressed using different words. For example, several translations use the term "sodomy" or "sodomites" when translating 1 Corinthians 6:9 and 1 Timothy 1:10. Young's Literal Translation (1862) uses the term "sodomites" in 1 Corinthians 6:9 as well as in 1 Timothy 1:10; the Darby Translation (1890) uses the same term when translating 1 Timothy 1:10. Clearly, if sodomy is banned, then at least male-to-male sexual intercourse was also intended to be banned.

Most of the other pre-1958 translations use the term "abusers of themselves with mankind" or derivations thereof. For 1 Corinthians 6:9, the King James Version (1611) uses "abusers of themselves with mankind"; the Darby Translation (1890) uses "abuse themselves with men"; and the American Standard Version (1901) uses "abusers of themselves with men." For 1 Timothy 1:10, the American Standard Version (1901) uses "abusers of themselves with men." The King James Version uses "them that defile themselves with mankind" (1611).

c. What is the meaning of the term "abuser of mankind" that appears so frequently in the older English translations?

The Middle English Dictionary was compiled in 2001 as a comprehensive analysis of lexicon and usage for the period 1100-1500 AD. According to this Dictionary, the first definition of the term abuse ("abusen") is "(a) To misuse (sth.) ... (b) to abuse (sb.) sexually (as by incest, sodomy, prostitution)." Thus, the older translations that use the term "abuse" would necessarily prohibit male homosexual acts where sodomy is involved.

The Oxford English Dictionary, like the Middle English dictionary, also includes the term "misuse" in the definition of the term "abuse." The second definition of "abuse" is "[w]rong or improper use, *misuse*, misapplication, perversion. *spec.* The non-therapeutic or excessive use of a drug; the misuse of any substance, esp. for its stimulant effects" (emphasis added). According to the Middle English dictionary, the second definition of the term "misuse" is to "To misuse (parts of the body, their function or beauty) sexually; to debauch (a woman); *to use (a man or woman) homosexually*" (emphasis added). Thus, homosexual conduct is implicated in the older translations of the Bible that used the term "abuse" or "abuser" of mankind.

Of course, the term "abuser" can mean much more than homosexual in this context. It can be one who "use[s] (a man or woman) homosexually," just as it can mean a pervert or one who misuses the function or beauty of the body in a non-homosexual way (*e.g.*, rape, pedophilia, etc.). Yet the point here is that Dr. White's argument—the appearance of the term homosexual only in the post-1957 translations demonstrates a shift from previous editions—is flawed. The idea of homosexuality is encompassed in the phrases used by previous translations, yet because the word "homosexual" did not exist at the time, they were forced to use a broader term.

C. CONCLUSION

In conclusion, it is natural that the term "homosexual" would not have been used in the Bible until the twentieth century, since it only came into existence in the late nineteenth century. It is similarly appropriate that the terms "abuser" and "abuse," and "misuse" would have been used in the earlier translations to signify the same thing, and that the Wycliffe Bible, published centuries before "abuser" and "misuser" came to refer to homosexuals, would have instead used "they that do lechery with men" to refer to the same concept.

CHAPTER 6. IS THE HOMOSEXUALITY IN THE SCRIPTURES DIFFERENT FROM THAT WHICH DR. WHITE DEFENDS?

The counterargument that Dr. White could raise is that even if "homosexual" is the correct translation of the terms in question, the kind of homosexuality condemned is not the kind that Dr. White advocates. His is a sexual relation between two men or two women in a loving, committed relationship—not between one man or woman who sexually abuses another person of the same gender. He is not, for example, advocating for homosexual pedophilia or other perversions. He may argue that a distinction needs to be made with respect to homosexuality, and the Scriptures only condemn harmful, not edifying sexual relationships. Homosexuality as an identity is never condemned in the Scriptures.

I have trouble accepting these arguments. If the homosexuality that Dr. White discusses is in fact distinct from the homosexual acts condemned in the Bible, God could have made the same known. Rather, we are left with blanket prohibitions of "unnatural sexual relationships" between women or between men, without any distinction as to those that are moral and those that are immoral. It would be an act of a cruel God not to highlight the distinctions if there were any. When God declared, "you shall not lie with a male as with a woman" (Lev 18:22) He could have added, "unless your condition was created such that doing so is natural for you, and you are in a loving, committed relationship." Rather than placing a blanket ban on sodomy in 1 Timothy 1:10, He could have issued more narrow prohibitions.

CHAPTER 7. THE TEACHINGS OF APOSTOLIC TRADITION

If Dr. White is correct asserting that Old Testament prohibitions on homosexual conduct do not apply to contemporary Christians and that modern translations of the New Testament erroneously place a ban on homosexual conduct, then the Church throughout its history must have been mistaken in its interpretation of Scripture.

A. THE TEACHINGS OF APOSTOLIC TRADITION ON HOMOSEXUALITY

The writings of the Church Fathers, as well as other sources of Apostolic Tradition,[7] have understood homosexual behavior to be sin. Basil the Great wrote, "He who is guilty of unseemliness with males will be under discipline for the same time as adulterers" (*Letters* 217:62 [A.D. 367]) and warned monks to "shun the companionship of other young men and avoid them as you would a flame. For through them the enemy has kindled the desires of many and then handed them over to eternal fire, hurling them into

---

[7] Designated "Sacred Tradition" in the Catholic Church, "Holy Tradition" in the Orthodox Church, and "Apostolic Tradition" in the Anglican and other Protestant Churches.

the vile pit of the five cities under the pretense of spiritual love" (*The Renunciation of the World* [A.D. 373]).

Eusebius of Caesarea writes: "having forbidden all unlawful marriage, and all unseemly practice, and the union of women with women and men with men, he [God] adds: 'Do not defile yourselves with any of these things; for in all these things the nations were defiled, which I will drive out before you. And the land was polluted, and I have recompensed [their] iniquity upon it, and the land is grieved with them that dwell upon it' [Lev. 18:24–25]" (*Proof of the Gospel* 4:10 [A.D. 319]).

B. THE TEACHINGS OF APOSTOLIC TRADITION ON EFFEMINACY

The Fathers similarly rebuke effeminacy among men. Cyprian of Carthage writes of the "abominations, not less to be deplored, of [m]en [who] are emasculated, and all the pride and vigor of their sex is effeminated in the disgrace of their enervated body; and he is more pleasing there who has most completely broken down the man into the woman. He grows into praise by virtue of his crime; and the more he is degraded, the more skillful he is considered to be" (*Letters* 1:8 [A.D. 253]). Novatian writes of the Jewish law that "rebukes men deformed into women" (*The Jewish Foods* 3 [A.D. 250]). Clement of Alexandria writes of the "disease of effeminacy" of one of the men among the Scythians (*Exhortation to the Greeks* 2 [A.D. 190]).

C. THE TEACHINGS OF HOLY TRADITION ON PEDERASTY

At the time of early Christianity, homosexuality was manifested in Greek society as the sexual union between men and boys (pederasty). This particular form of homosexual union was similarly condemned by the Fathers. Clement of Alexandria wrote that "conversation about deeds of wickedness is appropriately termed filthy speaking, as talk about adultery and pederasty and the like" (*The Instructor* 6, ca. A.D. 193) and he describes the sin of the Sodomites to be "fall[ing] into uncleanness, practicing adultery shamelessly, and burning with insane love for boys" (*ibid.*, 8).

Justin Martyr also writes, "You shall not commit murder, you shall not commit adultery, you shall not commit pederasty, you shall not commit fornication, you shall not steal, you shall not practice magic, you shall not practice witchcraft, you shall not murder a child by abortion nor kill one that has been born" (Didache 2:2 [A.D. 70]).

CHAPTER 8. THE CHURCH IS SLOW TO ACCEPT "NEW TRUTH"

Dr. White may make counter-argue that the writings of the Church fathers are not dispositive, as they reflect outdated views that do not recognize new truths on homosexuality, namely, that it is a gift from God. He writes: "the church has always been slow, if not the last institution on earth, to accept new truth."

Dr. White's notion of "new truth" is not in keeping with sound Christian doctrine. Jesus proclaims that He is the Truth ("I am the way and the truth and the life" Joh 14:6) and the Apostle Paul declares Him to be "the same yesterday and today and forever" (Heb 13:8). The doctrines of individual Christians may change over time, but the central tenets of orthodox Christianity do not change. The Apostle Paul warns believers not to "be carried about with various and strange doctrines" (Heb 13:9), but instead to search the Scriptures for truth.

Yet even if we were to ignore all of this and to accept Dr. White's contention that truth changes, how can new truths be distinguished from new falsehoods? If novelty is the sole criteria for truth, then why should Christians reject translations of the New Testament that incorporate the term "homosexual," since these translations are newer than the original translations that do not mention the term? If novelty is the sole criteria, then certainly these newer translations are truer than the old.

CHAPTER 9. HOMOSEXUALITY: "NATURAL"?

Dr. White states that "organizations representing 1.5 million U.S. health professionals (doctors, psychiatrists, psychologists, counselors, and educators) have stated definitively that homosexual orientation is as natural as heterosexual orientation," and leaves only a citation to "Recommended Resources, p. 23-24," which in turn leaves only the contact information of a list of organizations that are supposedly on Dr. White's side. I am not convinced. If Dr. White is going to say that reparative therapy is "based on an understanding of homosexuality that has been rejected by all the major health and mental-health professional organizations" (p. 22), then he ought to include specific references to the publications in which these organizations reject reparative therapy and why they consider reparative therapy a "danger." Furthermore, I would like to see how such organizations explain the apparently fulfilling lives that many former homosexuals live as a result of their conversions to heterosexuality. I have personally met several such individuals, including Melissa Fryrear and Kermit Rainman of Focus on the Family, and found neither guile nor guise in any of their testimonies.

CHAPTER 10. THE PROPER ATTITUDE OF CHRISTIANS TOWARDS HOMOSEXUALS

What is the proper attitude of Christians towards homosexuality? It is important to first remember that Christ died on the cross for homosexual and heterosexual sinners alike. The man engaged in heterosexual sin is, along with the man ensnared in homosexual sin, equally in need of God's mercy. Both require God's forgiveness. The proper attitude thus begins with recognition of our own sins and thanksgiving that God has proven that He can set us free and forgive.

The proper Christian attitude also recognizes that forgiveness requires the repentance of the sinner. Christians should thus put their hearts into praying that God would convict homosexuals of their sin. When this leads to confession, we must pray that God would pour the rivers of his love into the lives of the repentant, transforming, healing, and breaking the bonds of homosexuality. In the same way that God broke down the will of Saul of Tarsus, and transformed him into the greatest missionary of Christian history, so too can He break the sins of homosexuality and release freedom, salvation, and restoration. In the struggles over this question in contemporary culture, every Christian must thus be armed with trust in God's Word, love of neighbor, and faith in God's power to transform.

www.ingramcontent.com/pod-product-compliance
Lightning Source LLC
Chambersburg PA
CBHW060949050426
42337CB00052B/3279